The Admiral's Voyage

Written by
VICKI LOW

Illustrated by
ANTHONY BRENNAN

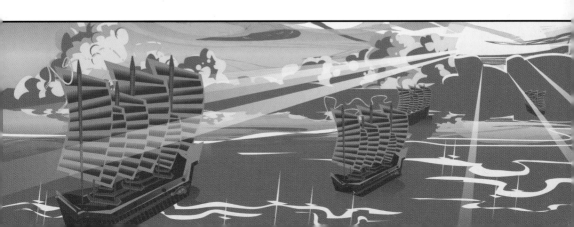

ZHENG HE

EMPEROR ZHU DI

MUSA

SITI

AH LIM

KING VIJAYA

MZEE

REAL PEOPLE IN HISTORY

ZHENG HE (1371–1433): The admiral who commanded the Chinese imperial fleet.

EMPEROR ZHU DI (1360–1424): The emperor of China who sent Zheng He on his voyages.

FICTIONAL CHARACTERS

MUSA: A nine-year-old boy from Sumatra who gets to sail on Zheng He's treasure ship.

SITI: Musa's elder sister who has a knack for sensing when trouble is on the way.

AH LIM: Zheng He's interpreter.

KING VIJAYA: The king of Ceylon who is taken prisoner aboard Zheng He's ship.

MZEE: An African villager who helps Zheng He find what he's looking for.

Contents

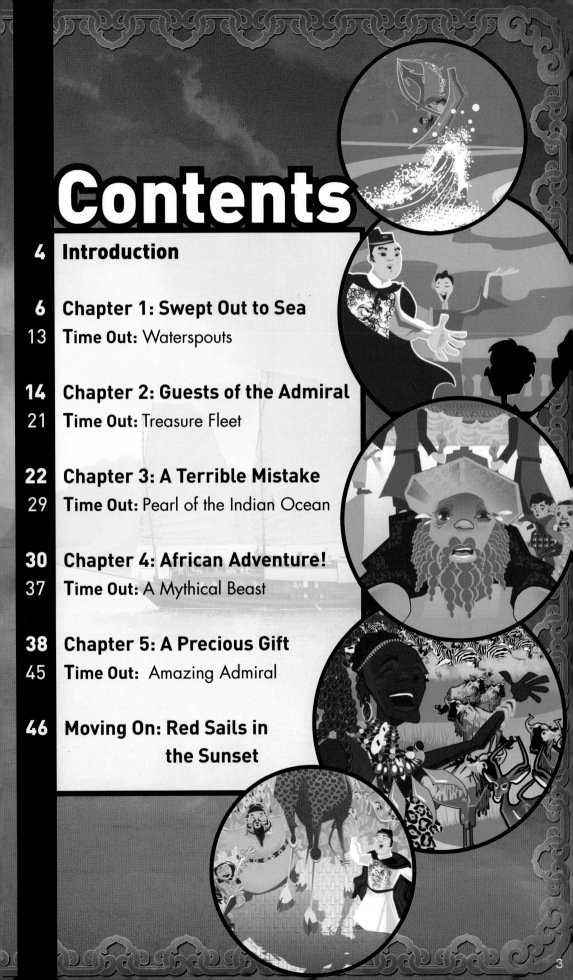

Emperor Zhu Di

In the early 1400s, a young man named Zhu Di (Chu-tee) became Emperor of China. Zhu Di was intelligent and curious. He was known as the emperor of "lasting joy."

Zhu Di wanted to explore the world and be known by other rulers. He ordered his workers to build a huge imperial fleet of ships.

Zhu Di sent his fleet out across the oceans almost a century before Columbus sailed for America.

The imperial fleet was a powerful force, but its missions were peaceful. Zhu Di exported fine silks, china, and items of gold and silver. His ships would return from their journeys loaded up with precious gems, ivory, pearls, medicines, rare plants, and unusual animals.

TIMELINE

1371 »	1402 »	1403 »	1405 »	1409 »
Zheng He is born in southwest China. He is captured and brought to the imperial court.	Zhu Di becomes Emperor of China. Zheng He is one of his close advisors.	Zhu Di orders a great fleet of ships to be built.	Zheng He leads the first voyage of the fleet. He sails to Vietnam.	The treasure fleet makes its second voyage — to India.

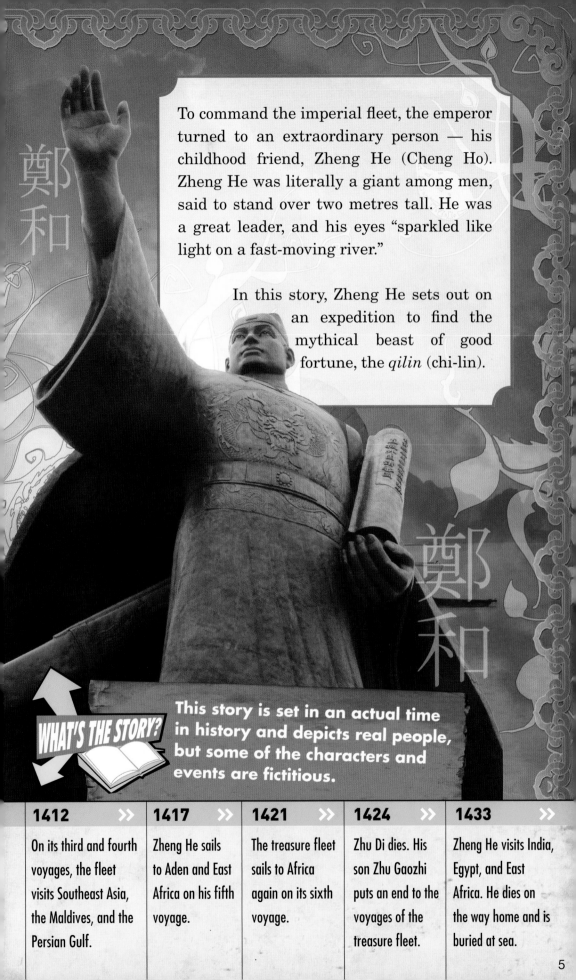

To command the imperial fleet, the emperor turned to an extraordinary person — his childhood friend, Zheng He (Cheng Ho). Zheng He was literally a giant among men, said to stand over two metres tall. He was a great leader, and his eyes "sparkled like light on a fast-moving river."

In this story, Zheng He sets out on an expedition to find the mythical beast of good fortune, the *qilin* (chi-lin).

WHAT'S THE STORY?

This story is set in an actual time in history and depicts real people, but some of the characters and events are fictitious.

1412 »	**1417** »	**1421** »	**1424** »	**1433** »
On its third and fourth voyages, the fleet visits Southeast Asia, the Maldives, and the Persian Gulf.	Zheng He sails to Aden and East Africa on his fifth voyage.	The treasure fleet sails to Africa again on its sixth voyage.	Zhu Di dies. His son Zhu Gaozhi puts an end to the voyages of the treasure fleet.	Zheng He visits India, Egypt, and East Africa. He dies on the way home and is buried at sea.

WATERSPOUTS

A tornado that forms over water is called a waterspout. Waterspouts can form when currents of cold air blow over warm water. The warm air rises from below and twists in the air, turning into a spout.

Waterspouts can be up to one kilometre high and 50 metres across. They travel across the water at speeds of up to 25 km/h. The winds that form the spout may be spiralling as fast as 95 km/h. Most waterspouts last only a few minutes.

Waterspouts may be the cause of some very strange weather events. In August 2000, for instance, it "rained" fish in Norfolk, England. In June 1997, hundreds of toads fell out of the sky onto the Mexican town of Villa Angel Flores. People think these fish and frogs could have been sucked up by a waterspout and rained down on land!

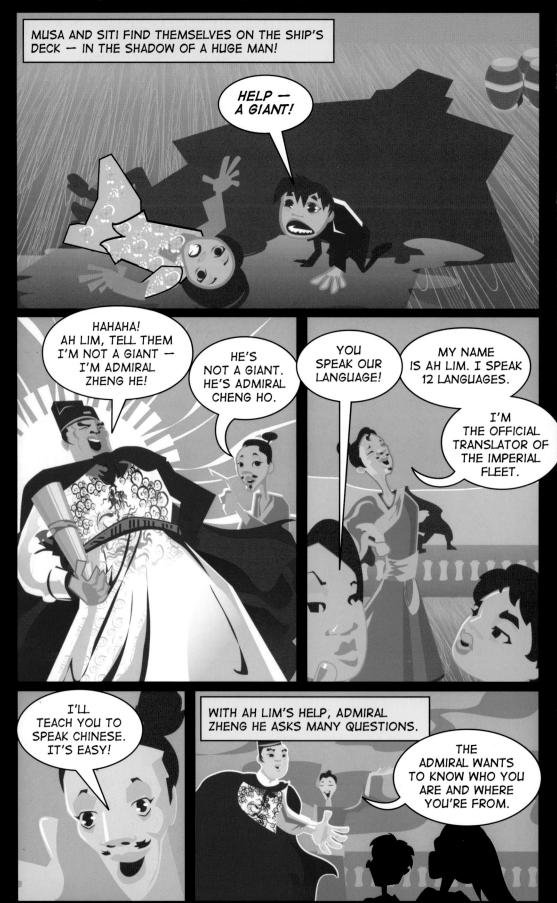

I'M SITI, AND THIS IS MY BROTHER MUSA. WE'RE FROM SUMATRA. WE WERE BLOWN OUT TO SEA.

AHA!

IF YOU ARE FROM SUMATRA, THEN YOU FOLLOW THE SAME FAITH AS THE ADMIRAL — THE GREAT RELIGION OF ISLAM!

VERY PLEASED TO MEET YOU, ADMIRAL!

THANK YOU FOR SAVING US.

AH LIM DESCRIBES THE MISSION OF THE IMPERIAL CHINESE FLEET.

THE EMPEROR OF CHINA HAS SENT THE ADMIRAL TO EXPLORE THE SOUTHERN AND WESTERN SEAS.

"THE EMPEROR WANTS THE KING OF EVERY COUNTRY TO RECOGNIZE THAT CHINA IS THE GREATEST COUNTRY OF ALL."

AH LIM TRIES TO TIE HIMSELF DOWN ON THE SHIP'S DECK.

HUH? I CAN'T FIND THE OTHER END OF THE ROPE!

OKAY, THIS SHOULD DO. NOW FOR THE OTHER END ...

SUDDENLY, A BIG WAVE WASHES OVER THE DECK!

AH LIM! NOOO!

GLUG! GLUG! GLUG!

TREASURE FLEET

Zheng He's fleet of ships was unlike anything the world had ever seen. It consisted of more than 300 ships and was manned by a crew of 28 000! The crew on these epic voyages included 180 medical officers, two secretaries, 10 translators, and an astrologer.

Zheng He himself sailed on a nine-masted *baochuan* (treasure ship). These treasure ships were the largest wooden sailing vessels ever built — four times the size of Christopher Columbus's *Santa Maria*.

The other ships in the fleet carried troops, horses, food, and water. The ships communicated with one another using lanterns, bells, drums, flags, and carrier pigeons.

A replica of one of the imperial ships

AFTER SAILING A FEW MORE DAYS, THE FLEET ARRIVES AT THE BEAUTIFUL ISLAND OF CEYLON, NOW KNOWN AS SRI LANKA.

THE CHINESE VOYAGERS PAY THEIR RESPECTS TO THE KING OF CEYLON, KING VIJAYA.

PEARL OF THE INDIAN OCEAN

TIME OUT!

India

Ceylon

The ancient island kingdom of Ceylon was located off the southern tip of India. Shaped like a teardrop, it was called the Pearl of the Indian Ocean.

Ceylon was a rich and fertile island. It was famous for its precious gems, spices, and tea. The beauty of Ceylon drew visitors such as Alexander the Great, Marco Polo, and Ibn Battuta.

Adam's Peak

The people of Ceylon followed the great faiths of Buddhism, Hinduism, Islam, and Christianity. In all these religions, the mountain called Adam's Peak was a holy place. People believed that a depression at the summit was Buddha's footprint — or Shiva's, or Adam's, depending on their religion!

Ceylon was colonized in turn by the Portuguese, the Dutch, and the British. It became an independent nation in 1948. Today it is called Sri Lanka.

WE'VE HEARD THERE ARE MANY EXOTIC ANIMALS HERE. OUR EMPEROR IS VERY FOND OF COLLECTING RARE BEASTS.

THE ADMIRAL DESCRIBES A *QILIN*.

IT HAS HORNS ON ITS HEAD AND HOOVES ON ITS FEET. IT IS A PEACE-LOVING, PLANT-EATING ANIMAL.

HMM, I THINK I KNOW SUCH AN ANIMAL.

THE NEXT MORNING, MZEE LEADS ZHENG HE'S PARTY ON A SAFARI — AN EXPEDITION TO LOOK AT ANIMALS.

YOU MUST ALL BE AS QUIET AS POSSIBLE.

YOU WILL SEE MANY ANIMALS FROM THE TOP OF THE HILL.

THE SPLENDOUR OF AFRICAN WILDLIFE!

A MYTHICAL BEAST

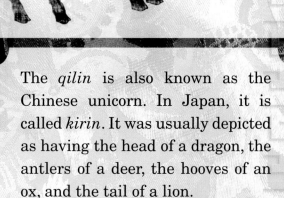

The *qilin* was a creature of Chinese myth. It was a good omen that signalled the birth of a wise man or the reign of a kind and able ruler.

Being a peaceful creature, the *qilin* did not eat meat. It was so light on its feet it could walk on water. It was usually gentle, but in the presence of an evil person it would show its fury by spouting flames from its mouth.

The *qilin* is also known as the Chinese unicorn. In Japan, it is called *kirin*. It was usually depicted as having the head of a dragon, the antlers of a deer, the hooves of an ox, and the tail of a lion.

When Zheng He brought a giraffe back to China with him, the Chinese really thought it was a *qilin*. The giraffe's appearance was just as the legends described!

THE ADMIRAL SHOWS OFF HIS MAPS TO SITI, WHO HAS LEARNED TO SPEAK FLUENT CHINESE.

SO THESE CHARTS TELL YOU HOW TO GO BACK HOME?

YES, MY DEAR. THEY TELL ME IN WHAT DIRECTION TO STEER AND FOR HOW LONG.

WILL YOU TAKE US HOME ON YOUR WAY BACK TO CHINA?

OF COURSE, WE'LL TAKE YOU HOME. BUT DON'T YOU WANT TO MEET THE EMPEROR OF CHINA?

MEET THE EMPEROR? OH, YES!

THE *QILIN* ISN'T FEELING TOO WELL, HAVING EATEN TOO MUCH *BOK CHOY*, A KIND OF CHINESE VEGETABLE.

BARF!

WHAT'S THAT STRANGE GURGLING SOUND?

GUR-R-RGLE

IT'S COMING FROM THE *QILIN'S* STOMACH!

EEK! SOMEONE WILL HAVE TO CLEAN THAT UP. I HOPE IT ISN'T ME!

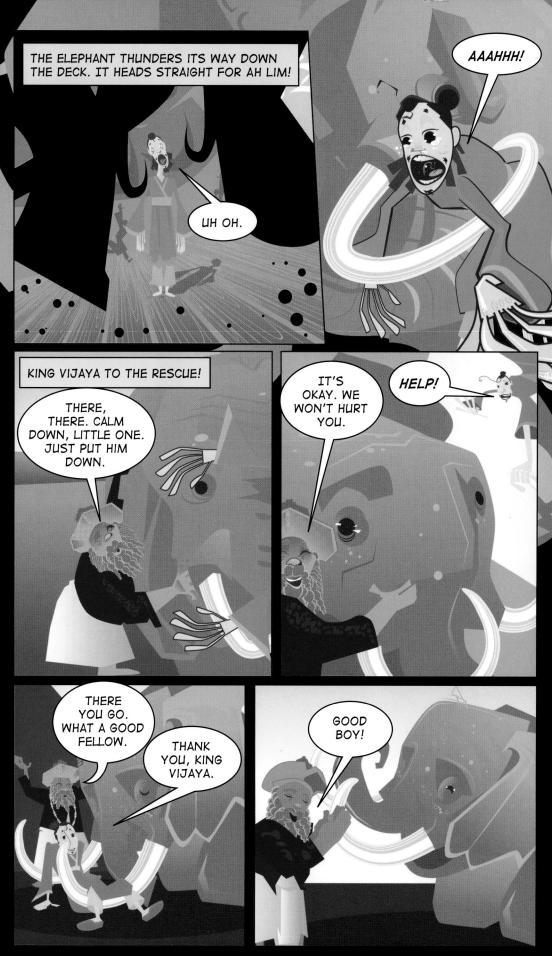

TIME OUT!

"He was two metres tall and had a waist about 1.5 metres in circumference … He had glaring eyes, teeth as white and well-shaped as shells, and a voice as loud as a huge bell."
— *Description of Zheng He in a 15th-century account*

Zheng He was one of the greatest seafarers in history. He was born to a Muslim family in a landlocked region of southwest China. Zheng He was captured as a child by Ming dynasty troops and brought up in the royal household with Zhu Di, the future emperor.

Zheng He became one of Zhu Di's most trusted officials. He led the imperial fleet on all its seven voyages, sailing as far as the Middle East and Africa. His many visits to Southeast Asia impressed locals so much that, to this day, he is revered as a saint throughout the region.

Red Sails

The voyages of Zheng He brought great fame, knowledge, and riches to China, but they were also extremely expensive. At the same time as these voyages took place, the Forbidden City (where the royal family lived) was being built in Beijing. The people of China endured heavy taxes to pay for these projects. When Zhu Di died in 1424, the country was almost bankrupt.

The next emperor of China put a stop to the imperial voyages. Relations with foreign rulers weakened, and China was closed to the outside world. A few decades later, Portugal took over as the mightiest seafaring nation.

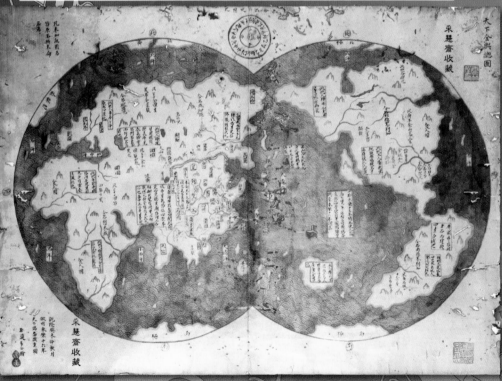

Map that supposedly proves Admiral Zheng He reached the Americas

in the Sunset

Five hundred years later, Zheng He's legacy endures. In Southeast Asia, he is regarded as the patron saint of the Chinese. In East Africa, there are people who believe they are descended from Chinese sailors of Zheng He's time.

We know about Zheng He's voyages across the Indian Ocean from records kept at the time. Scholars think he might have sailed to Australia, too. Recently, some have even wondered if Zheng He sailed to America before Columbus did. What do you think?

INDEX